Provocative is a Girl's Name

PROVOCATIVE IS
A GIRL'S NAME

MIMI FLOOD

Querencia Press, LLC

Chicago, Illinois

CONTENTS

Bark like a Dog

"Are you sexually active? Why not?" "You have a boyfriend? If I was your boyfriend, I would have sex with you every day." "Why don't you bring those nice lips over here and suck my dick" "Nice tits" "Shawty caking." "I'll fucking kill you!" "You could do porn and get away with it!" "Fuck you!" "Hey baby, can I get your number?" "Don't be such a bitch, get in the car." ***masturbating jesters*** " where you going?" "don't dress like a slut if you don't want to fuck" *weird animal sounds * "Really liked it better when you were bent over." "Aye, MA!" "I have a very large dick." ***dog whistle*** "Bitch!" "I love fat bitches!" "Can you do that?" ***shows pornographic image*** "Give me a smile and I'll leave you alone." "Well, you are cute, baby. Maybe don't walk alone anymore." ***follows you for ten minutes *** "Ayyy girl! How much??!" "I bet you already know how to please all the boys." "Your voice sounds like you been sucking dick." "Hey baby you're so sexy!" "We won't hurt you." "I would love to make you scream." "Cunt!"

THE VIRGINATOR, THE VAGINA SLAYERS

Ask you if you're a virgin / tell you how fuckable and perfect you are /

Give you an excerpt of how they're an immersive experience / you will never forget.

Usually cum once you sit on it.

Love Has an Entrance

Love can pump you up full of pills and forget to take you to the hospital.

Love can crash into you just before seeing the headlight.

HEADLIGHTS

Do you think about me as she crawls across the floor into your lap and gazes up at you with

Bambi eyes? When her hair falls onto your face and lips, does my face flash before you? At the

Auditorium where you held my hand when the speaker for drunk driving talked.

You knew of what happened to my father and the way a hit and run affected him. We were ten. I

Re-met you at fifteen in the back seats of the auditorium where there was an S.T.D lecture. I started to

Laugh because I thought of the Mean Girls scene, where the gym teacher says *don't have sex because you will*

Get pregnant and Die! You wrote *hi* on my thigh, with a blue pen, in a hole in my jeans. You were my still

Point where the rest of the world just moves. I always saw you, imagined you as the boy who stood in

My room with a halo. I loved you. I made love to you. I fucked you. I fought you. I hated you. I crawled

To you. Do you think about me as she crawls across the floor into your lap and gazes up at you with

Bambi Eyes, just before the headlights turn on?

Party

Do you want to go to a party? We can fuck in the bathroom / have unlimited free booze / I don't want to grow pretty / I don't even know what that means / pretty / be good / cross your legs / stick a needle in your eye / go to a place and hide / I will have the gore of all of it / my body soaked in blood / and have you lick it off.

Men's Testimonials

- If a girl is ran through, then she's for everybody else. Guys care about body counts because we want them for ourselves. Her body count number has to be a 0. She's got to be a virgin. I want to take that and show her what it's about.

- I don't mind body hair, but it's not what I go for.

- Women with short hair turn me off.

- A loose woman is for the streets.

- I think you have to take a tampon out every time to pee.

- If women don't want to be pregnant, then they shouldn't have sex.

- Statutory rape isn't a real thing if the girl is acting older than her age.

- Women just can't think rationally like men can.

- Every woman has a 'rape fantasy'. It's a natural part of being a woman.

- Can't you just hold it in? (Regarding period blood)

- Typically, I like to date women who are much younger because women usually peak around 25.

- My daughter is banned from using tampons. I don't need that taking her virginity. She will get used to having a penis inside her.

- Women who are overweight are unattractive (says the unattractive themselves).

- Getting an IUD doesn't hurt, and period cramps don't hurt that bad.

- Rape isn't possible if the woman won't let it happen.

- You can still get an abortion the moment a woman is giving birth.

- Women don't crave sex like men do.

- Is the vulva the hood of the clitoris?

- Condoms are a scam. They don't prevent anything. And you should learn to take a few risks.

- I fake putting a condom on, they don't feel the difference.

- If it isn't planned then I'm okay with one free pass abortion. Plan B is fine, I've bought them many times.

- I ask my girl if she's bipolar when she's being emotional and argumentative.

- I poked a hole in a condom so my girlfriend would get pregnant and wouldn't leave me.

- Eating out a woman is disgusting. Stuff comes out of there.

- You can't know you're a lesbian if you haven't had sex with a guy yet.

The Y

Chromosome

I once read a man felt a woman's vagina
Was so close to her anus that it
Was displeasing to him and that
Her confidence and ego should be shattered
For thinking they're all that.
I once read a man felt a woman could control
Her period, so when his coworker said she
Needed to go to the bathroom, he said she
Could control all of that, maybe set it aside till
About noon. I once read a man was in euphoria when
He would follow women to scare them
Without *actually* stalking them. But he was.
Do you know nipples develop in the womb
before embryos become distinctly male or
female, so by the time a Y chromosome
Kicks in to distinguish a fetus as male, the
nipples have already secured their place,
So they never had a chance to become
A female in the first place. But you were pretty damn close.

We are young gods / with soft skin / you leave your bite marks on my bones / they will be fossils at the MET / some protesters with a mundane reasoning will sneak acid in and throw it / and you and me will disappear

THE WOMEN IN BLOOD

The woman comes out of the far distance.

Nude, it's what you like to like but also deny.

But she's covered in blood.

People like to throw around traumatized. That fetus is a human

And experiences feeling, trauma.

A ten year old girl was raped by her stepfather and denied an abortion

Do you think she's traumatized? Do you think she will suffer PTSD?

Do you think she will scream at night? Do you think her back will

Crack, splinter with a sound of a crying baby from a far or near after giving birth?

Do women's and young girl's rights matter? You want to have a debate? Our life isn't a

Debate. Our body isn't a law. Our life isn't a bounty. When we're born, we are objectified,

Sexualized, and denied. We don't fall into the pit, we dive.

And when a woman comes out of the far distance.

Nude, it's what you like to like but also deny. But she's covered in blood.

All the dogs got loose.

Running and hollering with open mouths.

If they were using their snouts

They would have known

It wasn't her blood.

ON YOUR KNEES

Get on your knees / open wide / I'm going to spit in your mouth / Plath taught me that /lickety lick lick / I'm going to wrap you in a rainbow full of kittens in prism colors / shoot for glass / you're the price of electric to me / you're the lithium underneath my tongue/ I take my time / with eyes wide shut / take my hand / I'll take your doubt, shadows, and burning houses.

INVASION OF THE BODY SNATCHERS

The body politics of the politicians /

The media / the billboards and magazines /

Social media likes and comments.

Everything on TV is dressed / in women with bloody knees and hands /
holding ourselves in a fetal position in our palms / ahahahahahahahahaha/
at our trauma / make it porn to sell it /suck me / make it glamour /
fashion fashion/ enter some mediocre celebrity to try to tie you around
their fingertips/ love it love it / here is a knife to make you perfect /
bloody mouthed and barefoot.

The Stages of A Girl

Screaming Baby.

Mouse.

The sound of a

blender.

Destruction of a Tornado.

Mother / Daughter

Blackberry juice running down her inner thighs / before the embryo I was a
bad omen / that hush hush with a finger up to your lips / the portrait of a
march night / the love, the hope, the dream / the glittery blue eyeshadow/
the hickey on the neck/ the art form of swallowing pain / the humiliation
of taking it / the boys, the men, the weather/the tampon underneath the
pillow / the heartbreak / the smiles / the pigtails / the giggle / the wrap of
a tiny hand with a finger.

STAR GIRL

Dancing around in your perfume like your star girl / I miss the version of me when I didn't care /

Laying in a field pretending I'm dead so I can hear vultures screech / in my mother's costume

Jewelry / opening my eyes to stare at the ceiling in a twin bed / thinking who would love me / what is

There to possibly love about me / as my fingers dig into my thighs / I'm just a product of my time

Conjoining itself / going back to a beginning that has already ended.

The Dollhouse

In the dollhouse, the door is tightly shut. There are secrets written in the walls and baby teeth glued in the floor. My father would rub his head on my mother's thigh like a dog for forgiveness, but I learned manipulative games from alley cats, and put the veil on after I had sex with a boy who unbuttons me, calls me sweetness, and says all the right words, but forgets to call me, but when I pee'd blood in the toilet felt like it accomplished something. I hid joints in ripped doll heads. Looked for hope laying on the floor with dirt fingernails and blood of a bitten tongue. Everything eats you bare till your heart turns blue.

Queenie

Cherry bomb lipstick / Bow thigh tights / contoured with purple eyeshadow / taking thermal selfies in a bra and panties, in Lil Kim's famous pose, in full size mirrors / set on a computer screen / I like fucking / I like masturbating / I like doing a sex tape in black and white / I like taking tit pics / I like viewing myself in a different perspective.

Little Fish and Masturbation

My hair is full of birds flying me everywhere / I pluck a starfish and let it suck on my nipples / and go for a swim in a red pool / cry tears of green paint / and light a rose bud and smoke it with the thorns between my fingers / I have little fish for eyes / I masturbate to Marc Rebillet / I like when a man can scream in key / I have bite marks on my bones / and it wasn't from love / or from someone else / but I will lie to protect me from you.

HOW COULD THAT ABUSER BELIEVE IT IS THEIR RIGHT TO HARM ANOTHER PERSON?

Why didn't **YOU** just leave? How could **YOU** have let this happen to them?

Who would even wait this long to report such abuse? What did **YOU** do for them react that way?

You were the one that made them mad. **You** both have problems! Why did **You** keep going

Back? Why did **You** marry them if they did this to **You?** Wasn't there any red flags? Emotional

Abuse is not a real thing. **YOU** let this to happen to you. **YOU** are being over dramatic, it was

Just a shove. I'm sorry, but you have called out of work too many times. We have to let you go.

It was an accident. **You** know them, this isn't who they are. It was a joke, I don't think it was to

Humiliate you. I mean **you** never said they did this to you before. **You** always seemed like you

Were happy. They love **you** so much.

4 MONTHS / 9 DAYS AGO

4 months / 9 days ago / 2pm / there were clicking pens and a clock that
kept getting louder and louder / my name echoed a small room / my legs in
the stirrups sent a chill up my spine/ I dreamed of a white house with glass
windows / white picket fence with painted flowers /a in ground pool / a
Labrador retriever we name doofus / a kid playing on the swing set / we are
both happy / we are both full of love / that day I remember you leaving me
a voicemail while drunk that you couldn't get your dick hard for some
random because she wasn't me / and repeating 5x that you loved me / I
remember how much you suckered me into that / I love you / I miss you /
things will change / I promise/ all I could think about was / the neatly
sewn blanket of little things you would wrap around me with / the bloody
fingers from picking up glass / the way you drove fast in a car talking about
dying / how you accused me of cheating and wanting to leave you / and the
S.T.D you swore I gave to you / the mind fuckery / the push against the
mirror hanging on the wall that cut the back of my head / the eggshells I
walked on while you were looking at me / I would search my phone for
someone that I needed, but all I had left were acquaintances that belonged to
you / nightmares of screaming flowers / flinching lights / my broken stuff
trying to glue itself back together / drowning in an hourglass of sand /
spitting teeth / me waking up next you / your last words in the voicemail:
you asking why / and I thought of us sitting across a table at a diner /
telling you I found out I was pregnant and instead of being over the moon
and filled with joy / I looked in our bathroom mirror and the thought of us
being parents / the thought of me being bound to you for life / made me
fucking sad.

HOME clinic ingredients

Table top /

The windows covered in cloth / /

Hydrogen peroxide next to cotton balls /

The placenta /

The fetus in a biohazard bag /

The dead woman

My body runs hot when fingered. My body runs cool when you rub my breast. My body has body hair. My body has an eating disorder. My body has scars. My body has cellulite. My body is a womb. My body builds bones. My body is lines, light, and shadows. My body is a burrow. My body is a bitch. My body rots. My body gives you a dream. My body is a scandal. My body is a political playground. My body is a throwaway behind a dump or a river. My body is a product. My body is a used condom. My body is for a fuck. My body is bruised. My body is a whore, a slut. My body is fat. My body has bad skin. My body bleeds. My body has sex. My body has an orgasm. My body, my hip dips, and thick thighs. My body is cared for. My body is a diary. My body is art. My body is a religion. My body is a dollhouse on fire. My body feeds the porn bots. My body is bait. My body has a pit of anxiety. My body is a peacemaker. My body has a mouthpiece of a choir. My body has a venmo link for feet pics. My body has a peephole for when I need a break. My body is loved. My body is beautiful. My body exists and for that reason it is good enough. My body gives you presents of rage.

When I scream it sounds like a lullaby.

Pink

Peonies / bubblegum / Himalayan salt / a star burning naked / a fluttering amateur showing you her pink / pepto bismol / ballet slipper / cotton candy / a panther's pink tongue licking a silk sheet / I'll show you how much of an angel I am / and say I'm going to fuck you like a porn star / because that's what you would like / I'm taught to know what you would like / my wet pink rose / my sweetness of Venus / lick my honey that you created / I'm a vein of chaos / in soft skin / areolas / vagina / clit / pink

THIS HAS BEEN BROUGHT TO YOU BY A TAMPON X COMMERCIAL

I wish I could pull out my sadness like a blood-soaked tampon/ throw it as far as I can and run as fast as I can, till I can't breathe. You ever feel like a haunted house? Sometimes I think I'm going to walk past a grave that's mine and some lady is going to be standing there throwing *God Saves* pamphlets on it because she knows I'm not supposed to be there. But I'll just stand there with a midsommar end type of smile.

Pretty Girls Make Graves

And pretty girls make graves / they sizzle like butter in a frying pan / we thrive on instincts / there's always dying girls in bars / you touched me once and I think I died / we are the virgins / the fuck / the bitch / every version you conducted in your brain / the fat ass / the wet thighs / smooth lips / the silence / the secret / the scream / I'm not the dead girl in the swimming pool / I was never beautiful drowning / I was just gone

THE SECRET INNER WORLD OF GIRLS WHO FALL IN LOVE WITH EACH OTHER THAT'S NOT SEXUAL AND WATCH EACH OTHER BEND TO THE WORLD.

She was like pink frosting and hellfire / we would get ready for parties in dresses and panties we stole from Forever 21 / she would softly put lipstick on me / it felt intimate / like a communion of vulnerability / we hid ourselves in the bathroom laying in the tub with a bottle of vodka / asked each other, are we going to make it / practiced giving blow jobs on Popsicles / went skinny dipping with our boyfriends / and talked about our discharge after sex like it was a psychic reading / set lsd on the other's tongue / screaming with our bodies out of backseat car windows, feeling free and alive / We were like ambulance sirens and people chasing a storm / holding each other's bloody hands and dancing with a fist / cracked each other open to feel the air inside us / we gave our hearts to one another / loved each other like animals would, without second guessing.

LIPSTICK ON THE MOON

Our hair French braided around each
other's wrists / our dresses intertwined
/ rooted in dirt / we float in the
warmest blue / everything is going to
change / as we become parallel / we
stare into the sun / we leave our red
lipstick imprints on the moon

Cyntoia Brown, Brittany
Smith, Pieper Lewis,
Maddesyn George, Chrystul
Kizer, Chanel Miller,
Lauren Smith-Fields,
Annie Le, Catherine Susan
Genovese, Gabby Petito,
Gwen Araujo, Rebecca
Schaeffer, Emma
Sulkowicz, Vanessa
Guillen, Simone Biles,
Jessica Alva, Evan Rachel
Wood, Gabrielle Union,

Marissa Alexander, Jane Britton, Elizabeth Smart, LaVena Lynn Johnson, Miya Marcano, Blanca Luna, Sasha Lee Shah, Tshegofatso Pule, Amina Said, Sarah Said, Jholie Moussa, Raneem Oudeh, Judy Malinowski, Katie Piper, Christy Sims, Iana Kasian, Justine Gross, Naomi Skinner, Brianna Michelle, McKayla Maroney

"Boys Will Be Boys"

"What were you wearing?" "Were you drinking?" "Did you scream?" "Did you fight back?" "She should have enjoyed it." "How would you know, you were drunk, and you can't recall things accurately." "What did she think would happen, the way she was flirting with him?" "Women like that just regret having sex and are attempting to cover up their bad decisions by calling it rape." "Men have these biological urges to rape. They just can't help it." "I know him. He's a really good person who would never do something like that. She's only trying to make him out to be a bad person because he broke up with her." "You can't get raped by your spouse." "You are ruining his life. He has so much potential." "Did you say no?" "If someone doesn't want to have sexual intercourse, the body shuts down. The body will not permit that to happen unless a lot of damage is inflicted." "She's not the victim she claims to be." "You guys are friends, why would he date rape you? He is so upset by this, and I don't believe you." "How hard did you try to stop it?" "You always send mixed signals." "Was your door even locked?" "First he's beats you and now he's a rapist? Pick one." "Well if you were unconscious how do you know if you didn't consent?"

7 HOURS AWAY / 15 YEARS

He moved back to his hometown after he lost his job during a downsizing / 7 hours away / 15 years from the last day I saw him / His dad made his childhood room into a gym, so he slept on a pull-out bed in a semi-finished basement / shared it with the dog / he binge-drank in the afternoon for two months straight / went to the doctor for digestive problems / he started to dream of a blurred face woman sitting at the end of the bed / dead floating fish in a tank / racing heartbeats / woke up in a panic / after two months unemployed, still living with his parents on the pull-out bed with the dog / he got a job at a warehouse / $15hr / 40hrs a week / his mom was his boss / he finally quit drinking / started an online profile on tinder / the last picture is the one I took of him, 15 years ago / in front of an extraterrestrial highway sign two hours from a Vegas trip / Big smile in an alien costume / said he likes to laugh / climb / was looking for fun / had dreams of blurred face woman again but this time she was standing over him / dead birds dropping from the sky / bleeding trees and rivers turning red / eggs and bacon on a plate on the kitchen table covered in ants and dust / went to the doctor and got put on Xanax for anxiety / after meaningless hookups on tinder / he meets a woman at a coffee shop he frequents / and he likes her / this one is actually his type /

pretty with a sense of humor and a tattoo on her thigh / he reconnects with old childhood friends and makes some at work / goes to sports bars / goes to BBQ's / he's having fun/ leaves the warehouse job for a job he went to college for / 80k salary / gets his own apartment in a high-rise / with a king sized bed / he's happy / everything is perfect / but dreams of the blurred face woman / he takes a step towards her, and her body goes through his like a rageful offering, with weight against his body feeling like a ton / he wakes up with his shirt drenched in sweat / a racing heartbeat / choking on his airway / and remembers my face / my name / the morning I made you breakfast after you raped me

Mixtape

Bubble bath in a pretend mansion /overlooking a garden / cherry stems on the floor / the walls of the bathroom melt like fire to paint / I'm in a film noir / a Bettie Page in leather / I crack a whip and set blood in a cut on my thigh / and open a door to a 1960 Disney movie landscape/ I make out with Cinderella / and tell her to burn this town / hand her a match / I need noise so I step into an 80s club / and I dance until I see a man with a lost boys haircut and a cross earring dangling / whisper to myself [fuck] /with The Cars-moving in stereo playing/ we go to the bathroom and I watch him give me head and he fucks me from behind with my hands on the tank cover / He smiles after he zips his jeans and Breakfast Clubs me with his earring / once the stall door shuts after he leaves / I pop out of a tunnel in Super Mario Brothers / I get some coins and eat mushrooms / pop a bunch of goombas and go down a pipe / Come out on top of the moon / meet an alien who gives me a galaxy joint / we make moon angels / and eat the stars like marshmallows.

God Has My Bite Marks

I bit God in the throat / somehow I'm fourteen again / trying to break through my body and skin / with fat blaster pills and a shard of a wine glass / the boy I want / wants someone else / I felt hollow and had sex / left my panties on a crucifix nailed to the wall as a gift / I'm making space inside me for you / I'm swallowing the blood that I drew / you can't get out / too much rot for you to get out / I'm fourteen again / and I look for my mom to tell her I'm thinking about dying again, but her bedroom door is closed

WHAT Do You WANT TO BE WHEN You ROT?

Do you know bumblebees fall asleep in flowers? And they like to roll around in wooden balls / and can recognize you if they see you enough. My mother drove to a beach in a blizzard when she was young / just to see what the snow looked like on a beach / I thought it was the most poetic thing I ever heard / I dreamt of being with her seventeen-year-old self /dancing around in the blizzard / I think I was a twin and I ate her before an ultrasound / I feel she lives in an alternate universe where the mirror is a door to glimpse in. / I had a dream about a psychic / everyone in the room was talking loud /he told everyone to shut up and that we were all going to die / next thing, I'm in his car making out with him / and we stop as the car starts to go fast with his foot on the brake / we're both screaming / it's dark / it's snowing / I go through the window /over the cliff/ go through the ice / the deeper I went, the cold morphed into warmth and I saw sun crystal rays in the water going through my body / then I woke up / I wrote a poem about cherry blossom trees in springtime, it was a message in a bottle for cum on my face / I read it in class, but I liked how it got lost in translation. I like when you're standing still and everything moves fast and you can't make it out / Do you think people actually like their friends? / Or do you think you just share the same likes and dislikes and hard knocks of life, so it's just easier to call yourselves besties / Or even childhood lifers. I always wonder why they couldn't let go of one another / be free. / Maybe I'm just a hard shell. Or jealous of it / I have 89 acquaintances. I met some through elementary, work, someone I met from so and so for 3hrs, another workplace, and trade school / They seem kind, but I don't feel like getting to know them on a personal level / Maybe it's because I'm always afraid they will leave me in some way. I feel like a voyeur in their lives on social media / I feel you should pick your flowers in a field with the root and bulb and say, look here is my heart. Feel the thorns. The stem. Everything is always wrapped in newspaper or cellophane or something. There's no feeling. I want raw. I want substance / What do you want to be when you rot? I think I want to become a home for something.

PERVERSION

I'm a diabolical perversion / I like fishnets and sex / biting necks like a wild animal / I'm hysterics and pills / a speculum and blood clots / I'm an angel that smiles with bloody teeth.

The Walking

Erection,

The Walking

Contradiction

Just because we fuck doesn't mean I trust you or even love you.

I'm not the one that will call or send cutesy texts with ♥ ⬭

Sometimes you're just the erect

That was easy.

Good Vibes Only

My vibrator is the cure.

SEARCH LOADING.. .. ..

Why are daddy issues bullets against women

Who didn't have their fathers to show what a good example

Looks like, but your pornhub history shows cum on mommy?

DINNER PLATE

Eat it up.

Lick it up.

I devour it all

Into oblivion.

Into biting on

My fingertips till

It starts to bleed.

Why do I make

Everything

Into a matter.

Little Doors

Little doors on my body / open up and you'll see / a sleepover with
everyone sharing a single pint of ice cream watching Now and Then/
making out with a friend for pictures to put on Myspace /getting head for
the first time / crying in a bathroom / being alone in a room / taking
pictures in crop tops with no panties / being alone in a room / sitting at a
desk / being alone in a room / floating around in a pool where the other
Substitute bodies are beneath

I SCREW BETTER THAN GOD

Was I the angel in the poem you wrote / was I something that you could never figure out / was I the girl with the bra full of condoms / a half smile / tinsel heart / did you have me undress / did you sign my body with your tongue / was I the nocturnal flower that bloomed its petals just right / could you fuck me with only poetry / I screw better than God

banana

Crying to Beethoven / peeling a banana / with chocolate syrup running down / you wanna make out? / You wanna braid me into your body? / You wanna scream till you have nothing else to give? I'm your favorite TV show / your favorite channel

Fallatio

Big eyed

Quiet girl

Swallowing pearls

White Dress

Splash it with red paint

Set handprints all over it

Rip it with a knife

Cupid Heart Shaped Pupils

In a cupid dress and gloves in baby pink / I have heart shaped pupils / that get arrows when I get excited / and I plucked the stars from the night sky and placed it on my eyelids /people's wishes turn into confetti underneath my fingernails and I have glitter in between my inner thighs so lovers lips are marked / scented with vanilla perfume / everything shocks when I touch it / with a kind of spark that takes a minute to come back down / for me it's when my tongue touches yours when we passionately kiss / the world is one bruised grapefruit hanging by a hair, spinning, and I bite it / tongue it / squeeze it as the juice drips on my chin and fingers / falls on my bare chest / the music I play is too thin for these walls / missing tiles on the floor / and cracks on the ceiling / vibrating my body in every direction / waiting for the walls to crumble around me into light ash / the kind you can catch / I stick my finger in a red Jell-O round cake that my grandmother makes every Christmas since the 1960s and look at it like its stuck in amber / look at it with a tilted head like it's something interesting / something timeless / I want to be love in an enigma / no / I am love in an enigma / a beating heart in an embryo of a cloned animal / the sound of whipped cream /a sizzling fire opal / the making of a rainbow / a dream come true / the name of a storm / the vessels in your eyes shooting electricity down your spine / your starlet with big hair and a smile that's so tragic with that one single tear running down the cheek / your angel in black thigh high leather boots, with an oversized Cruella coat, lighting your cigarette / your final girl that isn't a virgin from the beginning of a horror movie / Everything will always try to swallow you whole /more than once / more than you can count /get to it first / with a controlled exhale and relaxed fingers.

It Was a Wednesday

When I tried to kill myself it was a Wednesday / I thought about jumping
off a bridge a year prior / I envisioned / my fingers dancing on the bars and
the cold air running through my body like a ghost and feeling razor-sharp
shark teeth when I hit the surface, and then the thought just disappeared/
On Tuesday I was fine / I went for a morning run / went to work / talked
to my mom about seeing her on the weekend / went to a friend's party /
laughed and danced / saw all the videos posted on TikTok / When I woke
up / I went to the bathroom / opened the mirror /saw something / there
was no real thought out plan or why / I took it and passed out / I killed
myself and woke up / I vomited on the carpet / I cleaned up my mess and
took a shower, sitting long enough for my fingers to prune / nobody knows
/ people stand and walk through that spot / all I see is my ghost body / I
try to avoid it / it's just another crammed memory told in my point of view.

Lamb

I forgive myself with the blood of a cherry on my white cream blouse / the stained jelly on my fingertips / / the blood on my panties / we didn't say much / even when I walked on glass and had bloody footprints along the white clean floor tiles / I practice saying words in a mirror / hope, grief, home, loss,loss, fuck, fuck,fuck. I just want to scream / We swallowed our agony in smiles and laughter in crowded rooms / I saw a pool, went in to sit at the bottom on a November night / I wanted you to sit with me. /hold my hand / I had a dream down there / I found a lamb. It looked tired. It tried to stay alive until I could hold it. /and it looked like it was in peace when I felt the last exhale. / I was waiting for you to tell me you didn't love me anymore / but both of us were exhaling silence

IRIS

Did you know your iris could leak out of a hole in your eye if the proper trauma was inflicted? I would scratch at my face out of nervousness / I wanted to carry the least amount of myself /you know how people wear bugs that are fermented in necklace pendants? I want do that after I die, be around someone's neck like a timeless artifact / like a friendship noose of two missing puzzle pieces /you know some things are stolen before you notice they are missing / and some secrets are like a lament configuration box with a severed head / a dissection of pain and healing / you only show to a kind of person you have love for

Shape of a Girl

—After Joan Macleod—After Bjork

I'm a monster in the shape of a girl / a woman in the shape of a monster /

I'm made out of ungodliness and sharp teeth /

Hiding in girlishness

I'm a fountain of blood in the shape of a girl /

I'm better at holding a knife / than holding someone's hand.

this is for you,

you, my number one ⊡ah, ah, ah, oh yeah, yeah, yeah⊡

superstar lyrics by usher

Cum inside me

I'm so wet

You're so big

I'm cumming

I can't take it anymore. Let's just do anal.

Can I just give you a blow job?

Oh, God

Faster!

You are so amazing!

(Encouragingly with a splash of manipulation)

CLOTHESLINE

Wrung out all the bodies I have /some are animalistic / others are beauty queen in big curls and a plastic crown / shygirl in journals and overalls /emo punk with pink hair and a nose ring / slut era, good time girl, wearing a heart choker and lace dresses / Hung on a clothesline to dry / then folded nicely in a drawer.

The Imaginarium and the Dome of My Cranium

Once every couple of years I get a drunk voicemail from my estranged father.

I want someone playing a saxophone to be out on a terrace with me sometime around midnight in light rain while I drink wine.

I grow feathers back from men who plucked and collected. Thinking I can never fly.

I was nine when I found out people are replaceable.

Sometimes my stomach contracts after cumming.

I wonder how a caterpillar species that can turn into a snake when threatened knows what a snake looks like.

I can be the bird in the dog's mouth or I can be the dog.

I like yearbooks with imagine if.... they had me as imagine if I was loud ...and I was—inside my head I was screaming.

I want to live in a Lisa Frank cover: riding a rainbow over a pink and purple dolphin.

I've adopted names since I was kid. I think my favorite is Stariza.

Female vampire bats will share regurgitated blood with their girlies if they found they missed a meal.

I want to have just a feather boa around me on a roof top, with the Eiffel Tower, it's lights blinking behind me while I'm dancing.

Sometimes I think I'm as meaningless as a Bible in a motel dresser

Do you ever see a house that's a replica of someone you cared about in another town? It's like a living breathing haunted house in live form from your memory right to the red door.

In my hair there is a used condom, a friendship heart locket, a razor, black lipstick, flower buds, wishbones, ribbons, old concert tickets.

I want the end of my life to be driving in a pink convertible on a highway while blasting *Spitting off the Edge of the World* with ending credits and a dedication.

My best advice is whatever dies, live what remains.

PROVOCATIVE IS A GIRL'S NAME

Provocative is a pearl on her tongue. Provocative is her pink lips. Provocative is fishnets.

Provocative is a giggle at a church while you dream of being in between her thighs. Provocative is

Her mouth to papercuts. Provocative is her red dress. Provocative is handprints on her body.

Provocative is her laced up back. Provocative is her stare through you. Provocative is her

Umbilical cord around her neck. Provocative is her bloody nose dripping onto the porcelain sink.

Provocative is a conch shell, a split papaya, a flower. Provocative is a perfume. Provocative is her

Glasgow smile. Provocative is a used sanitary pad uncovered. Provocative is an infinity symbol, a noose

For two, girlhood and womanhood. Provocative is bleach and dirt. Provocative is to hold knives shaped in a

Lipstick. Provocative enough to throw bible verses at. Provocative to be ruined by past men, but his hands

Are the ruin, instead of having palms that show love. Provocative is a god, begging to be believed on her

Knees, crying tears of blood, pointing to a cross, as everyone just stares and becomes a bystander.

Provocative is a girl's name.

CPSIA information can be obtained
at www.ICGtesting.com
Printed in the USA
BVHW050835080223
658123BV00026B/417